AF228923

WHAT ARE PRIMARY SOURCES?

SUSANNA KELLER

Published in 2019 by Britannica Educational Publishing (a trademark of Encyclopædia Britannica, Inc.) in association with The Rosen Publishing Group, Inc.
29 East 21st Street, New York, NY 10010

Distributed exclusively by Rosen Publishing.
To see additional Britannica Educational Publishing titles, go to rosenpublishing.com.

First Edition

Library of Congress Cataloging-in-Publication Data

Names: Keller, Susanna, author.
Title: What are primary sources? / Susanna Keller.
Description: First edition. | New York, NY : Britannica Educational Publishing, in Association with Rosen Educational Services, 2019. | Series: Let's find out! Social studies skills | Includes bibliographical references and index. | Audience: Grade 1–5.
Identifiers: LCCN 2018020597| ISBN 9781508107033 (library bound : alk. paper) | ISBN 9781508107224 (pbk. : alk. paper) | ISBN 9781508107392 (6 pack : alk. paper)
Subjects: LCSH: History—Sources—Juvenile literature. | Information resources—Juvenile literature. | Research—Methodology—Juvenile literature.
Classification: LCC D5.5 .K45 2019 | DDC 907.2—dc23
LC record available at https://lccn.loc.gov/2018020597

Manufactured in the United States of America

CONTENTS

What Are Primary Sources?

A primary source is a work that gives original information. It comes from a time being studied or from a person who was involved in the events being studied. Some primary sources supply facts about a subject. Other primary sources express the views of people who experienced events.

A secondary source does not give original information.

It interprets or summarizes information from primary sources. Textbooks, biographies, encyclopedias, and dictionaries are normally secondary sources.

A book about the American Revolution that was written in the 2000s is a secondary source. A journal that a soldier kept during the American Revolution is a primary source.

Sometimes, the way a source is used determines if it counts as primary or secondary. An article from the 1950s about Pocahontas isn't a primary source about her because she lived in the early 1600s. But it could be a primary source about how people in the 1950s viewed Native Americans.

Art like this wall painting in an Egyptian tomb is a primary source for studying ancient Egypt.

COMPARE AND CONTRAST

How are primary and secondary sources alike? How are they different?

Published Sources

Some primary sources are published **documents**. Publication is the printing of multiple copies of a document to be sold or distributed to people.

Newspapers and magazines are published documents. Articles in newspapers and magazines can be primary or secondary sources. If the author writes about seeing an event or gives an opinion about an event, the article is probably a primary source.

Newspapers are published regularly. They offer stories about local, national, and international news.

Documents are written or printed papers giving information about or proof of something.

Broadsides and pamphlets are primary sources that were commonly published in the past. A broadside is a single large sheet of paper with printing on one side. In the days before TV, radio, and the internet, broadsides were among the quickest ways to spread information. For example, during the American Revolution, colonists passed around broadsides of the Declaration of Independence. Pamphlets are brief booklets that promote a specific view or provide information. Pamphlets were among the first printed materials.

John Dunlap printed the first broadsides of the Declaration of Independence on July 4, 1776.

In Their Own Words

If you want to know how people in the past felt about the events they lived through, it makes sense to look at their own words. Several types of primary sources tell people's own stories.

Autobiographies and memoirs are books about the author. A memoir usually focuses on events and other people in the author's life. An autobiography concentrates on the life of the author.

Interviews let you know what people—some famous, some not—thought about the times they lived in. Oral history projects are collections of interviews, usually of people who lived through similar experiences. The Federal Writers' Project of the 1930s collected stories of former slaves. The American Folklife Center's Veterans History Project has interviewed veterans of many US wars.

The Veterans History Project has collected stories of veterans who served in US conflicts since World War I.

COMPARE AND CONTRAST

How are the stories in oral history projects like those in memoirs and autobiographies? How are they different?

Unpublished Sources

Not all primary source documents were meant to be public. Letters were written for the people to whom they were sent. Journals and diaries are personal accounts, made for the writer's own use.

In past centuries, people in public life often kept diaries. These writings have become valuable sources for historians. The private, candid views set down in personal journals help to show the full picture of an age.

During World War II, a young Jewish girl, Anne Frank, kept a diary for two years while hiding from the Nazis with her family.

These primary sources can give details not found in official records or books, which may have been **censored** during that time.

Manuscripts are another type of unpublished primary source. One kind of manuscript is the text of a book before it is published. Looking at book manuscripts shows how an author's ideas changed in the course of writing. Books that were written before the invention of printing also are called manuscripts. In the Middle Ages, monasteries produced handwritten manuscripts with fancy designs and miniature pictures.

In a manuscript from the Middle Ages, an illustration shows Noah's Ark in the form of a Viking ship.

Official Accounts

The original US Constitution is preserved in the National Archives in Washington, DC.

Governments and other institutions keep records of nearly everything they do. These official records include laws, court cases, treaties, constitutions, and censuses. A constitution is a set of rules that guides how a country, state, or other political organization works. A census is a count of the people who live in a country. Some censuses also tell things about those people — their

backgrounds, what they own, and how they live.

In ancient times, especially in the Middle East and China, governments kept lists of kings and wars. They also recorded events such as the building of temples and natural disasters. All these records are important primary sources.

Sometimes official records are discovered by chance. When Germany was defeated in World War II, the Nazis left behind many documents. Historians have used these primary sources to describe the history of Germany between 1933 and 1945.

THINK ABOUT IT

Why do you think governments take censuses? How might censuses be used?

Informative Images

Some primary sources are images, not words. These sources include drawings, sketches, photographs, cartoons, and maps. They give information about people, places, objects, and events that words may not be able to describe.

Newspapers and magazines have printed drawings and photographs of people and events since the 1800s. Advertisers and businesses use photography to show people their products.

This photo of New Orleans was taken in 2005. It shows the flooding in the city caused by Hurricane Katrina.

Cartoons are drawings that make a point, tell a joke, or tell a story. Political cartoons criticize the government or make fun of it. These cartoons are usually single drawings, but there are some political comic strips.

Maps are drawings of places. Topographic maps show the location and shape of features on Earth's surface. Political maps show countries, states, provinces, counties, and cities.

This 1915 cartoon is about women gaining the right to vote in Western states, before women in the East.

Think About It

What kinds of information can images show better than words?

Audio and Video

President Franklin D. Roosevelt spoke to the American people in radio broadcasts known as fireside chats.

Audio (sound) and video recordings can be primary sources, too. Examples include movies, TV and radio shows, news broadcasts, and music.

Some of the oldest video primary sources are newsreels. Theaters in the early 1900s showed these short films about current events. Early audio primary sources include recordings of ordinary Americans playing folk and blues music, made in the 1930s.

Since those times, many important speeches have been recorded. Between 1933 and 1944, US president Franklin D. Roosevelt delivered a series of radio addresses, called fireside chats, to explain his policies to the American people.

The first radio station started broadcasting in Pittsburgh, Pennsylvania, in 1920. Within two years, hundreds of radio stations opened. Radio was a major source of information and entertainment until the mid-1950s. Then television became more popular. Today, podcasts and online videos are common sources of information.

Today, people can watch videos on a range of devices, including computers, phones, tablets, and TVs.

COMPARE AND CONTRAST

How are audio and video sources similar? What advantages does each type of recording have?

ARTIFACTS

We can learn a lot about the past by studying documents, photos, and recordings. However, some cultures did not leave these kinds of primary sources behind. Not all cultures use writing. If you want to study these cultures, you need to look at other kinds of records, such as artifacts.

Artifacts are objects made by humans. They can tell us things about the time when they were made.

These artifacts of prehistoric peoples were collected in Yellowstone National Park.

The earliest stone tools are artifacts. So are the household objects thrown in the trash today. Everything made by human beings—from simple tools to complex machines, from the earliest houses to modern skyscrapers—is an artifact.

Sometimes people in the present aren't sure how people in the past used a particular artifact. In those cases, researchers try to interpret the artifact, or figure out what it means.

THINK ABOUT IT

If historians from the future saw your room, which artifacts might they have trouble interpreting?

Go Right to the Source

Primary sources have a number of uses. Reading the words written by people in the past, hearing their voices, or seeing what they looked like can bring the past alive. Primary sources make it easier to understand that people in history had beliefs, hopes, and dreams, just like people do today.

This old photo of a smiling Navajo woman reminds us that people in the past had full lives.

Historians use primary sources to write about past events. When they do, they make interpretations. They choose which events or which people to focus on. They give their own ideas about the causes or consequences of events.

When you look at primary sources yourself, you become the historian. Primary sources can help you to interpret what happened in the past, why past events were important, and what the past means to people today.

This family looks at primary sources in an exhibit about Rosa Parks, a leader of the civil rights movement.

THINK ABOUT IT

The saying "history is written by the victors" means that people who conquer others get to tell the story. Do you think this is true? Is it fair? Why?

Consider the Creator

It is important to remember that the people who created primary sources had their own points of view. For every primary source you look at, think about who created it and how that person relates to the information provided. For example, a person's knowledge depends on their education and experience. Also

Signs for political candidates try to convince people to vote for that person.

consider how a person's background—their age, job, social class, race, religion, nationality, and so on—might affect how they see a situation.

Some primary sources make no attempt to be **unbiased**. Opinion pieces, such as editorials, are meant to convince others that something is true. Political speeches try to persuade people to vote for a candidate. Propaganda is information used to influence public opinion or even to change people's beliefs. Propaganda gives a one-sided message. It focuses on the good points of one idea and the bad points of another idea.

> **VOCABULARY**
>
> **Unbiased** sources are unprejudiced and offer a balanced view.

Challenges

Despite the benefits of using primary sources, they can be hard to work with. Many are written in languages other than English. Some have been translated into English, but many have not. Some are written in languages that are no longer spoken. A few are written in languages that no one alive knows how to translate. Even sources in English may be hard to understand because of the more formal way that people used to write. Handwriting styles from the past can be challenging to read, too.

The Rosetta Stone has the same text in three writing systems. It was the key to understanding ancient Egyptian hieroglyphics.

This piece of an Egyptian scroll is about a thousand years old. Parts of the scroll were damaged or destroyed.

Finding primary sources can be difficult as well. Countless documents and works of art have been destroyed over the years—some in fires or wars, some eaten by pests, and others because they became fragile and eventually turned to dust. It also can be hard to find primary sources for less privileged groups, such as women, poor people, and minorities.

Finding Primary Sources

Primary sources are preserved in many places. When possible, they are kept in their original form. Paper copies also may be made, or digital copies may be stored on computers. Important records are often collected in archives, museums, and libraries. Local organizations and religious groups also keep valuable records.

Records from long ago may be harder to find. They may have been written on stone or drawn on buildings.

The US National Archives preserves many important documents.

These primary sources may be buried in the ground, partially destroyed, or covered in layers of paint.

Historians who study ancient time periods work to uncover these records. For example, historians know about the laws made by the Babylonian king Hammurabi because the laws were inscribed on a stone pillar. The pillar, made in the 1700s BCE, was discovered in 1901. Historians also use the tools of **archaeology** to study ancient times. They gather information from the tools, homes, clothing, weapons, and other objects that ancient peoples used or owned.

Using Primary Sources

The study of history helps to make sense of humankind. It helps people to understand the things that happen today and to guess what may happen in the future. Many historians would argue that primary sources are the most important tools for these tasks.

A boy uses a stereoscope at the Pioneer Museum of Alabama. People in the past used this device to see photos in 3D.

These moccasins were made by Northeast Indians. What clues do they hold about the person who wore them?

Students of all ages can use primary sources to study a topic. A primary source can help students to think of many questions to explore. For example, examining clothes from long ago could bring up the following questions: What materials were used to make this outfit? Why were these materials used? Was this outfit worn in warm or cold weather? How often was it worn? Was it meant to be worn by a certain person?

Glossary

address A rehearsed speech.

archive A place in which public records or historical documents are preserved.

autobiography A history of a person's life, written by that person.

broadcast A single radio or television program.

candid Frank, open, and honest.

consequence The result or effect of something.

dictionary An alphabetically arranged list of words and their definitions.

encyclopedia A set of articles, published in books or on the internet, that provides general information about different topics.

inscribe To write, engrave, or print something on a surface.

interpret To explain the meaning of something.

manuscript A written or typewritten document.

miniature Very small.

monastery A place where members of a religious community live and work.

nationality A label that tells the nation or country to which a person belongs.

social class A group of people in a society who have similar roles and power.

translate To change from one language or set of symbols into another.

treaty An agreement between two or more countries.

veteran A former member of the armed forces, especially a person who served in a war.

FOR MORE INFORMATION

Books

Barrington, Richard. *The Magna Carta*. New York, NY: Britannica Educational Publishing, 2017.

Ciment, James. *How They Lived: An Annotated Tour of Daily Life Through History in Primary Sources*. Santa Barbara, CA: Greenwood, 2016.

Clapper, Nikki Bruno. *Learning About Primary Sources*. North Mankato, MN: Capstone Press, 2016.

Clay, Kathryn. *The Declaration of Independence*. North Mankato, MN: Capstone Press, 2018.

Jennings, Brien J. *What's Your Source? Using Sources in Your Writing*. North Mankato, MN: Capstone Press, 2018.

Paley, Caitlyn. *Slave Narratives and the Writings of Freedmen*. New York, NY: Cavendish Square, 2016.

Websites

Library of Congress: Kids and Families
https://www.loc.gov/families/
Facebook: @libraryofcongress; Twitter: @librarycongress

Primary Sources: A Research Guide
https://umb.libguides.com /PrimarySources/secondary

United States National Archives and Records Administration
https://www.archives.gov
Facebook: @usnationalarchives; Twitter: @USNatArchives

INDEX